Dedication

I dedicate this book to my wonderful family who have been so tolerant, kind and engaging in the journeys and adventures I have taken them on with animals, and to my grandchildren –that they may know the love of animals.

Acknowledgements

Writing this book has been so much fun and has in no way been a solo activity. I owe my patient, long suffering, fence building husband so much. He has listened to my thoughts, encouraged this crazy idea and lived each adventure with me.

I owe my love of life and nature and adventure to my extraordinary parents who taught me about seeing the good, working hard and loving the journey. They taught me to have integrity, to be resilient and to be courageous. Even whilst growing up in a war I was not deprived of the magic of childhood, play and exploration.

To my two crazy sisters who have always been there, during the dark times and the good, ready to play and laugh, I thank you for being you.

And my three amazing children who inspired my entire life and give me the gift of endless joy. Shane with his unbelievable inner strength, Deon with his complete determination and Krystal with her spirit of adventure and love of life. How they have blessed my very soul.

Thank you to the publishers of this book, for your expertise and time. For believing in me and feeling the spirit of the connection.

To those children who have suffered so much at the hands of cruel humans, who have touched my life and taught me humility and compassion – thank you.

To my other family – Roxy, Twix, Jellybean, Poppy, Tigerlilly, Simba and all the little fluffy creatures who have enriched my life. Thank you for your unconditional acceptance of my mistakes and failures as a "zoo" keeper. Especially Roxy, for all she has brought into my life and the lives of the children from hard places who come to visit. I will let you off for all your interruptions, shedding, chewing, eating and demands on my time. Thank you for having been my therapist.

Contents

Prologue

As a child, I thought that Gerald Durrell was this magical person who lived on the magical island of Corfu, so far from the dry plains of my African home. I grew up in the southern part of Africa in the landlocked country of Zimbabwe (formally Zimbabwe-Rhodesia, formally Rhodesia, formally Southern Rhodesia), where I learned to love nature and life. *My Family and Other Animals* by Gerald Durrell, was my entertainment on the somewhat limited rainy days. Children's TV in the 1970s was limited to half an hour a day of Spiderman (in black and white). The rest of the day was spent in the garden with my beloved dogs, Nandi and Chaka, along with dung beetles, ant lions and light green chameleons, which miraculously changed colour.

My two older sisters were often dragged into my adventures, although their passion for all things creeping and crawling was not as refined as mine. I was the youngest of the three. Shann, the oldest, was and still is a terrible tease and once told me that the only reason we had pets was for food storage, thus to eat them. This caused me the loss of gallons of tears and she received a good telling off. Cecily was the girly-girl of the bunch, who loved doing hair and make-up and didn't care much for my animal adventures.

My mother was the boss in the home and kept us all in line. She taught me to try everything, to enjoy life and to love the wildlife of our homeland. My dad was the careless adventurer who caused my mother many worrying moments. On a night following some flash flooding, dad decided that we would drive through a flooded river rather than wait until morning. Crossing the bridge in the dark African night was not a smart idea, as water crept into the foot well of the car. Nevertheless, we made it, as we always did with dad.

In Harare (formally Salisbury), we lived in Mabelreign, an area of big houses on the outskirts of the city. Our homes were surrounded by bush with a wild feeling about the place. Mauve Jacaranda Trees, orange Strelitzia and purple Bougainvillea coloured our lives. The area was hilly, which made my cycle ride to school a little challenging.

It seemed that half the land was filled with frogs, 'chongolols' (millipede of some great size and pronounced chon-go-lo-lo) and large African Land Snails, who carried their crunchy home proudly with them. As we rode our bikes to school we had to navigate through an obstacle course of these creatures. They did tend to come out after the infrequent rain, and any cars going before us did not seem to consider the results they left behind for us poor cycling kids to miss the crushed, squished and splodged remains.

Although our country was at war during my growing up years, it seemed that I had so much freedom. I went everywhere on my bike. To get to my best friend's house I would cross a vlei and have to dismount over a small gully, which was about two feet deep and one foot across. At this point in the path there was a nest of red ants, and since I only ever wore sandals, I was a prime target. It was quite a skill to balance on the pedals of the bike and make a leap from the pedal to the other side without putting my feet on the ground with a bike to follow. The return trip was harder, and I often landed in the path of these jaw-gnashing little red beasts. The survival instinct for me meant speed and agility. I would land in their territory and climb aboard the bike with feet flailing in the hope that those ants – that had not yet embedded their jaws in my flesh – would fall off, and those who had would lose their heads. If their bodies came off, then they stopped biting, so I would just have to pull their heads out of my skin. A gruesome tale, which was painful for me, yet deadly for them.

This was my world. A place of creatures, adventure and real life. My interest and love in all things that moved was established in this wonderful African place. However, the paradox for me was that not all children in my world had what I had. Leaving my home and travelling a short distance we would see the Shona children. They lived in mud huts and did not all go to school. They ran bare footed through the hot sand and made their toy cars from old wire fencing. Crossing the Limpopo River into South Africa on holiday we would be accosted by dirty, shoeless children begging for our empty soda bottles, as this would score them a few precious cents from the local store. There is an early memory of a small, dark-skinned girl sitting on the roadside with her mother weaving baskets. She had a dog – the ropiest dog you have ever seen – but they were friends. The dog lay protectively at her side and unmoving, an image that has stayed with me.

Now married with my own children and grandchildren, life has thrown many challenges and pleasures. Bob, my wonderful life companion and our children Shane, Deon and Krystal, have all shared in the learning and experiences that have brought me to this point: the point where my two great passions meet.

My two greatest loves in life – after my family of course – are animals and children. Children who come from hard places; hence this book and the Noah's Ark Family Project, which is where we work with animals to help children recover from trauma. It is almost as if my love of life, animals and my desire to help others, has at last found its place. Animal Assisted Therapy is now my passion. The human/animal connection that is so powerful to me is the key to connecting: creating that attachment we all need to survive.

The pages in this book illustrate a journey of an animal-filled life – where a connection has been made. Through this journey I have created a junction where my passions meet: helping children connect with life through creating a relationship using the unconditional gift of animals. My hope for you as you explore these pages is that you feel it. Feel the thrill and get the buzz of a connection being made with these kids as they learn what love is.

The Attack

It was a hot Zimbabwe day. All the windows and doors were open to allow even the smallest breath of air to bring some relief into our home. The African sun had passed its midday heat and was heading for the horizon when the first mortar hit nearby, followed by automatic fire. Years of preparation from caring, organised parents and we were in survival mode. "Stay below window level!" dad shouted. An interesting concept when you consider our Spanish-style house with large arched windows that almost reached the floor.

Dad's gun was now in hand and we were heading for the safety of the passage where there were no windows. Chaka (a large male Alsatian) and Nandi (a Keeshond cross Alsatian) went into protective mode. They stayed close to our sides within the confines of the small passage, a little unsure of where the danger was that they needed to protect us from. My young head was buried in Chaka's warm fur, feeling his breathing bringing a resemblance of comfort.

Chaka was unsure of what to do with rapid gunfire on the other side of our garden wall. I grabbed his collar as he tried to run outside to investigate, just as another volley of bangs exploded. He tried to run towards the door with my eight-year-old body in tow – my skinny, bare legs rubbing against the passage carpet. My sister was crying and Chaka was anxious. It seemed as if the terrorist attack would not end. I felt fear and was flooded with adrenalin, yet I had no concept of the danger we were really in. The Rhodesian war was part of my young life. I knew nothing else. The dogs wanted to protect but could not understand the risk and danger.

I buried my head in Chaka's warm belly again, blocking my ears to pretend that I could not hear what was happening. There was some sort of safety in this dog; he was my guard dog, my protector and my best friend. My life was full of running and playing with him. If I was careless and damaged mom's garden, Chaka was there with me when being told off, and then with me to put things right. He alerted me to the presence of snakes and scorpions. He trotted alongside my bike and rested at my feet when I sat for a brief moment. As Chaka shook with fear this day, I shook too, and together we huddled in the passage surrounded by big-eyed humans all experiencing that same emotion, feeling vulnerable, fearful, at risk and in shock.

I had previously observed the effects of a mortar bomb hitting a fuel depot and remember the mushroom explosion as we fled the area, running on young legs with my father's hand dragging me to safety. My inquisitive mind was in awe of the bright red and orange display rising above our heads and the heat singeing the small hairs on our faces. Yes, I was familiar with war and the activity of terrorists.

Voices could be heard. Were they the gooks coming into our garden? What now? Dad's small revolver wobbled shakily in his hand. What good this would have done against the automatic AK47 – one has to wonder – but dad would protect his girls. Hearts thumping and ears straining, the shouting conversation was in English. Dad carefully sneaked a peek through the corner of the window. "They're in our camo," he announced. The Rhodesian home-grown camouflage was easily identifiable for his trained eyes. "The boys are here," his relieved voice said. The army had arrived.

Climbing over our bundle of humanity and canine in the passage area, dad took the now brave Chaka to investigate. We heard him talking. There had been a terrorist attack on the house one up from ours. The suburban area of St Andrews Park on the outskirts of Harare was a spacious assortment of typical urban African homes, with large gardens, trees and un-edged roads with deep ditches to accommodate rainfall. Two houses along the road lived the Minister of Finance and his family.

Dad returned to tell mom what had happened and for some reason took me with him back to the incident. Hand in hand, with Chaka at my side, we walked down the road amongst the armed soldiers with their gigantic monster crocodile troop carrier, with its bulging green belly parked in my world. The terrorists had driven into our suburb with the single intention of killing our neighbour. Unfortunately, his young son was opening the gate at the time and he too was gunned down. My young eyes observed the trauma of a violent death. The father was hunched over his steering wheel and his son lay in a heap in front of the car. Death. So gruesome. So final.

I did not feel the pain in my own little body. I felt a sadness – a shock. Returning to my mother's arms I cried, with Chaka's caring eyes watching the human emotion as he nuzzled my hand. A sadness I could not understand. The pain – the very little pain I felt was real. Chaka's antics during the shooting had shaved the skin from my little leg. The nerves were announcing their existence as the leg-long graze began to throb and ooze. But I was alive. Chaka now stayed close to me and would not leave my side. He nuzzled up close to me as I cried. He slept by my sleeping bag on the floor as we all slept in my parent's room, now a place of safety for the family. He remained at my side protecting me, being my friend and companion. It was like we had had an extreme experience together. We had seen the frailty of life.

Moments like this are life changing. Why did dad take me – a young child – to see the foils of war: I do not know? But I learned about compassion. A respect for life – for childhood. I experienced the connection with a dog who knew I was in pain. It was one of those moments in life that profoundly affected my actions for the future. The integration of life – animals, fear, emotion, need and survival. This book is based on these experiences – the experiences of living in a world of beauty and distress and how to use one to cope with the other. Is it possible for the beauty of friendship between a human and a dog to be capable of aiding emotional survival? My experiences say "yes".

My Ark

The idea and establishment of Noah's Ark Family Project was not something that I had planned, but rather a montage of life's choices that led to this moment. Now an adult living in the UK we moved to a property to support my husband's sauce business and this property just happened to have fields and stables. Standing at my kitchen sink, I would look through the large window at these empty paddocks and wonder what I could have running free in that space. Being an African girl at heart, I wondered what would be required to have ostriches in Cornwall. A bit crazy I know, but it was a thought that led to research. Bob's entrepreneurial spirit joined in and he found a market for ostrich products from feathers to feet!

Now, I must tell you that many years before, Bob had brought ten baby chicks with the intention of having home-grown eggs. I cared from them from their small fluffy stage to adulthood. He then jokingly named them Roast, Curry, A La king, Peri Peri and so on. Much to his horror, just as they were about to start laying, I gave them to our gardener – there was no way I was going to eat these chickens I loved and cared for. My chickens come from the shop! So the idea of having ostriches for any other purpose other than pleasure was not an option! Pigs were another consideration, yet quickly rejected for the same reason.

Then I was offered a horse. An enormous white horse that was overweight and difficult to ride, but needed a new home. We went to meet her and the reality of caring for such an enormous creature was a terrifying prospect. But a seed had been planted in my brain. What about something a little less ''enormous'' and a little more "realistic". Driving around Cornwall now had new meaning and I would spy on all horse filled fields and look for something more my size.

Then it happened. A call came through from a friend who was aware of two young mini Shetland ponies for sale. An appointment was made and off we went. Oh my! I fell in love! What was not to love?

Simba aged 6 months
Photo by Deon Chorley

They were the size of a big dog – but so beautiful. Fluffy and cute – cute – cute! Learning to care for them was just such fun. My first experience of scooping poop from the field was met with helpful hooves that knocked over filled wheelbarrows, nibbled unprotected hay bales and broke into the carrot sacks.

Then Poppy joined the family and we were complete – or were we? Having these wonderful little creatures just filled my life with such joy. Krystal (my daughter studying at university) had a work placement at the RSPCA for her Zoological Conservation Degree and came home one day worried that they had three male Chinchillas that needed to be placed, but no one had sufficient space to accommodate them together. Chinchillas? I barely knew what they looked like, never mind how to keep them alive and healthy. But being easily swayed, I went to see them. Fatal! They are amazingly beautiful, entertaining and oh, so soft. They were brothers that had been together from birth and co-existed in this little family unit. Back to research and a major learning curve. Google is an amazing tool when you are committing to the care of foreign creatures.

"Chinnies" (as they became known) are very friendly if handled regularly; they are entertaining and have almost no smell. They do not cost a fortune to feed and have a long lifespan. So the application was submitted and the RSPCA process of inspection and questioning began. Bob's building skills were now being put to the test and a stable was selected. Special untreated wood and welded fencing purchased. It felt like we were preparing for a special delivery. The cage was designed to fill half a stable, high enough for humans to stand in and filled with layers of climbing limbs. This cage was a work of art.

The day of the inspection came and boy were they impressed! So much so that they returned to take photos to illustrate excellent Chinchilla husbandry! Wow! I sounded like I knew what I was doing! The next day we went to collect these fluff balls. This was the first time I had ever even held a Chinchilla. On arrival in their new home, they carefully left the cat carrier and explored their house, swings, bridges and sand bath. They were then named Haagen Dazs, Ben and Jerry.

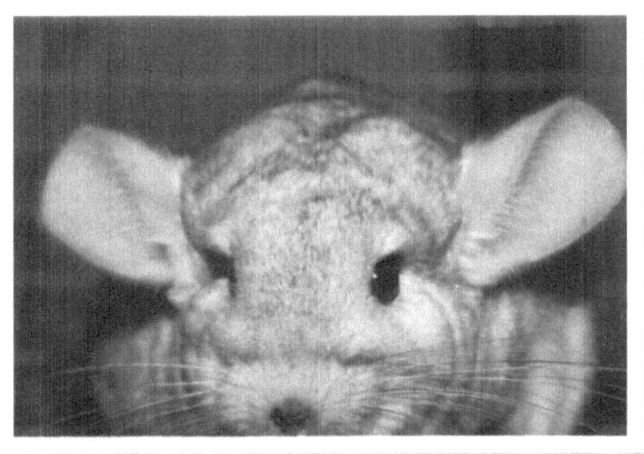

Jerry – A Chinny with attitude!

We soon learned about their characters. Haagen Dazs was Mr Sleepy and would fall asleep in the midst of any activity that was a little boring. Ben had freckly ears and was very friendly, and would do anything for a raisin. And then there was Jerry. He only had three legs. Apparently, he broke a leg catching it in a wire cage and the leg was removed. Watching him run around you would never know, but I think that he was still a little mad at the world. He had long rodent teeth that he knew how to use. Whilst his brothers were fantastic when being handled, Jerry needed bite-proof gloves and a strong will!

As my mini zoo was being established, I found that when I told people about these creatures they would ask if they could bring over their children. It became a common activity in our home to introduce the animals to people, and I was watching the pleasure they experienced when interactive with the animals. The therapeutic value was so evident. We were building skills, self-esteem, causing laughter, serotonin and endorphins were being generated.

We decided that we needed to fill some of the other stables, so we went on a mission to find two female rabbits and two female guinea pigs to live together. The idea behind this project was to help children in foster care to see that families that are different still work together. To create a link for them to learn from. The animals were purchased and hand reared so that they were all very happy to be handled.

Then one evening we were cleaning out the stables when Krystal appeared looking bewildered. She called me into the rabbit and guinea pig stable and there in their little wooden house was a white baby! One little white baby rabbit. I have been told that it is difficult to tell the difference between male and female rabbits, and I guess this is true. So the "daddy" was segregated and had an emergency vet visit, and the baby was christened Snowball.

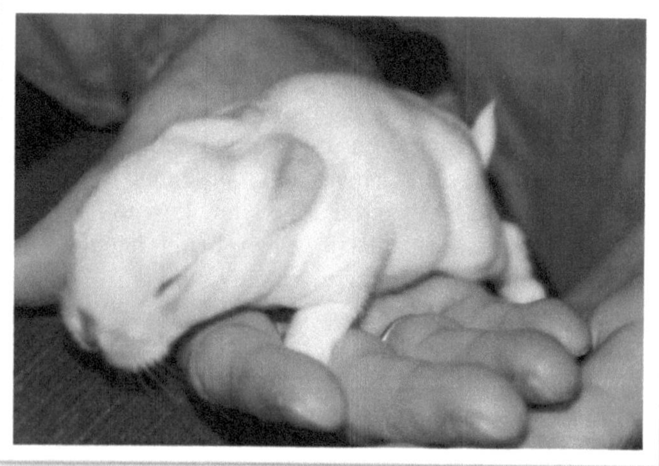

Snowball

I was now finding that I was being approached by professionals I worked with to see if I would work with troubled children they were responsible for. Children who were finding it difficult to connect with humans, yet who had an affinity to animals. My professional work with children placed me in a unique position. And then the penny dropped. I could continue to work with these kids but use animals to enhance this work.

We sat up late one night as a family and agreed the name and the logo. Noah's Ark had always been a story that I loved as a child – filling a boat with all types of animals and having an adventure. I could not think of anything that would be more exciting than that. Policies were written, insurance purchased, animal's care professionalised and website built. *Noah's Ark family Project* was created.

Then Bob came home with the news that he knew of three chipmunks needing a home. Woo Hoo! Chipmunks – why not! So off we went to Penzance to increase our menagerie. There were three hyperactive little creatures in a tiny bird cage. Having no idea how to handles these little critters, we researched on the smartphone on the way home. There was not too much to know really, but handling them was interesting. We stopped to buy a larger temporary cage to accommodate them, whilst Bob's building skills could again be improved. But getting them from the bird cage to the temporary cage was a little challenging. Once safely in their new home, and knowing no better, we closed the clip door having had a successful transfer.

Standing at the kitchen window that evening, a strange movement caught my eye. A little bouncing body with a fluffy tail was joyfully bounding across the roof of the stable. Yes an escapee! Oh gee! Was it possible to catch an escaped chipmunk? Probably not, but I was going to try. Broom in one hand and fish net in the other, I ran to the end of the stable hoping to corral a chipmunk. Family members were shouting instructions and informing me in high-pitched voices of every step he took. Three animated ponies now galloped between the excited humans. He then stopped and looked at me, considered his actions, and then turned around and bounced back along the stable roof and disappeared into the stable he had escaped. Human shrieks filled the air. "He is in the stable!" "Get him!" "Close the door!" "Block the holes!"

We snuck into the stable and, with the door still open, there in the temporary cage were three chipmunks, looking at us with innocent eyes. I learned that the little clip mechanism that worked for birds and hamsters simply did not work for chipmunks.

With the stables now filled and the fields being used for free running ponies, I felt a completeness. A new daily routine filled the little spared time I had. Managing a large charity in an emotionally charged field like domestic abuse took so much energy, and coming home in the evening usually meant that I was done for the day. But now I had a new set of responsibilities to energise my tired body. Mixing feed, mucking out, grooming, collecting eggs, stroking and handling these precious mammals was hard work, relaxing, de-stressing and rewarding.

On many occasions I have been smartly dressed in preparation for a high level meeting, and a colleague would come up to me and remove a piece of straw from my hair or coat. I remember special moments when I have been called in to work at night due to an attempted suicide or child protections case, and having finally arrived home, Poppy has neighed a welcome from the darkness of the field. Or when Jelly Bean rested his soft body in my lap and meowed until I had moved my tapping fingers from the keyboard and attended to this attention seeking cat. I have always felt uplifted by these very simple experiences.

I was on a major learning curve. Not only about how to keep all these animals alive, healthy and happy, but also how to use these wonderful creatures to benefit others.

Back to Google and tapping away to learn about social lubrication, animal assisted activities and using animals in therapeutic sessions. This was an interesting journey that kept leading to one thing. Dogs seemed to be the animal used in the majority of settings, even though most domestic animals are considered. My research then naturally turned to dog breeds, nature, temperament, ability to learn, social engagement with humans, desire to please and playfulness. One breed kept gaining my attention. The Golden Retriever is used to help the disabled, sick, blind and for hospital visits. Their affable character attracts humans, and they never get tired of being in your company and are always eager to please.

I continued my research by accosting retriever owners in the street, asking them about their dog's character, the best food to use and how to keep their fur soft. Every engagement I had with one of these dogs enhanced my mood and stole my heart. The search for a suitable puppy began and a trip to Devon was undertaken to see a twelve-week-old litter.

Roxy was in my lap, nibbling my fingers and rolling into my arms, exposing her soft, white tummy. She selected me and a match was made.

Roxy became a beautiful, light-cream adult, who was the best tool in my tool kit. Loved by the children I have worked with, she was playful and attentive. She would welcome them warmly, play when they wanted to play and would happily lie down to be groomed, manicured and examined by little fingers. She would relax when the stethoscope was used to listen to her heart or when her paw was used to make a clay or ink print. She would retrieve anything you threw and has delighted all with her water games.

When Roxy rested her beautiful, soft, warm chin in my lap, my fingers would seek out her curls in her neck and massage her silky ears. I always felt uplifted by her desire for my company, her desire to interact with me – a human.

All pet owners who have a bond of attachment with their pet will know the feeling of unconditional love, friendship and acceptance they receive from their animal companion. This connection is foundation for Animal Assisted Therapy and the motivation for Noah's Ark. To share this connection with children from hard places is simple and rewarding for all involved. I have experienced reciprocal pleasure with the child and their carer when the child first touched a chinchilla or gave Roxy a command and she obeyed. These experiences that pet owners understand can be healthy, therapeutic and just great fun.

The Elephant Parent

The row of 1970's cars began to gather in the sun and dust of Sinoia, a small town outside Harare, Zimbabwe, known for its spectacular natural shaft cave filled with cobalt, crystal clear water. The convoy was set to leave on the hour and the military vehicles were placing themselves in the front, middle and back of the line of civilian cars. The young, armed soldiers came to each car to ask about what weapons were in the car. Information was shared about specific areas of risk where the terrorist presence was most active and that under no circumstances should we stop in these spots. If we were attacked we were to hold the convoy and keep driving with non-drivers having use of available weapons.

My sisters and I paid little attention to this drama; as girls growing up in the Rhodesian war, this was part of life. My sisters – being older and wiser than me – were more excited about checking out the uniformed talent than worrying about being ambushed by gooks (colloquial term for terrorist). Whilst all this was going on, I sat in the boot of the station wagon with the large window rolled down surveying the African vlei for the common zebra and wildebeest grazing nearby.

All cars were started and the convoy was underway. There was a tension in the air and for my parents this was a big deal. Previously on this same road, on the 3rd September, 1978, the Hunyani passenger flight 823 Viscount was flying from Kariba to the capital Salisbury (now Harare) when the ZIPRA guerrillas using a surface to ground missile hit the aircraft forcing an emergency landing in the cotton fields. The plane cartwheeled and flipped on impact with thirty-eight people instantly losing their lives. Ten survivors were rounded up and massacred by terrorists with automatic gunfire, leaving others who had managed to survive, to hide in the thick African bush. This event shook our small country; however, my parents did not believe in giving into the fear factor of terrorism, so we continued with our planned family holiday at Caribbea Bay Resort at Lake Kariba.

The veldt eventually gave way to rolling hills as the convoy approached Karoi and this was the place. The place where we had previously seen them. The massive grey bodies that lumbered through the bush grazing and destroying as they moved. The first time I had seen an elephant was when a herd crossed this very road two years earlier. My heart pounded as the mother, adolescents and babies commanded their way over the tar strip and into the roadside bush, their tusks leading the way with babies frolicking behind.

This was a pivotal moment in my life. I think I fell in love. Many of my childhood hours were spent in drawing and colouring elephants. One of my childhood heroes was Viv Wilson, who ran a wild animal orphanage called Chipangali in Bulawayo. He hand reared many calves rescued after culling. His video footage of the rescue of animals when flooding the Kariba Valley stays with me today as does the news footage of the 600 elephants culled by the Rhodesian Wild Life Management. The sight of the carcass recovery and piles of ivory being weighted and cleaned ready for international trade horrified my young mind. All this was prior to the CITES ban against the ivory trade.

There was outrage and approval. The elephants were too numerous that the land could not sustain them. But they are magnificent creatures with a right to live. They enrich our planet and teach us humanity and compassion. They are the animal that is debated by governments, conservationists and royalty. They have the greatest impact on our environment and yet are the most human in their emotional capacity. They share with us common emotions and they have a parallel lifespan. Their development equates to ours, and they demonstrate attachment in families, sisterhood and maternal connections. Their babies cannot survive for the first two years without suckling and they reach puberty between ten and fifteen years. We have seen their family reunions and the mourning of a death. They are loyal and caring and they demonstrate many things that may be diminishing in our human society.

They seem to have more than we do in some capacity. Their ability to remember, navigate and communicate surpasses our own. They have the largest brain of any land animals and have three times more neurones than an average human. Whilst many of these neurones are used to manage their large bodies, their mental capacity seems to surprise and enthral those who study them. They have the ability to use tools – breaking off a tree branch with their trunk and using it to swat files, pulling up tufts of grass with a clump of mud attached and hitting against their feet until it is mud free – illustrating coordinated use of their own bodies. They can smell water in dry river beds and skilfully dig, creating a pool that will feed them and other thirsty animals.

As a child on that African day, I noticed the caring elephant mothers – mothering that seems to be lacking in many human homes. Their great size and gentle ways seemed contradictory.

Female elephant are very maternal. They develop a strong attachment with their calves. From birth they are attentive, gentle and caring. After delivery they are often seen to assist the new-born to stand up or walk. The baby will seek protection under its mother's belly when fearful or threatened, and the mother will be very defensive of her young. The size of the calf makes it vulnerable but the mother seems aware and does not trip or step on the baby. If a calf strays too far, the mother will bring it back. She will assist and support her young by pushing or holding them as they go up and down the slippery bank of the watering hole or keep them upstream of themselves whilst crossing rivers. These relationships between mother and calf are life-long as their matriarchal clan consists of mothers, adult daughters and all their offspring.

For the first two years of a calf's life, mothers are not only attentive but calves are disciplined by their mothers with gentle shoves, pokes and slaps and will sometimes be given a stroke or touch of the trunk for reassurance. Mother and calf maintain a close distance to enable constant touch. These mothers are nurturing and patient and their actions seem natural and unconsidered. They demonstrate a desire to communicate, protect and show affection towards their babies. They are steadfast, consistent and serene. She will support her young over pits and holes, using her body to protect the young from the sun or predators. She will bathe the calf by spraying with water and then gently scrubbing. If the calf squeals in distress, the adults will rush to protect and defend. It is not surprising they create a lifelong attachment.

The young are also overseen by their aunts, older siblings and other family members. Play, interaction and socialisation within the herd is as vital as sustenance for a calf. Elephants form deep family bonds and live in tight matriarchal groups of related females. With these large brained animals with long lives the young brain takes time to develop, and in the case of elephants the young gain much knowledge from imitating their mothers. Joy, anger, grief, compassion and love are amongst the complex thoughts and feelings that create their emotional attachment.

These exceptionally social animals are capable of experiencing psychiatric trauma. During many culls, helicopters have been used to buzz overhead and round up the herd. When all the adults were shot, the young were left traumatised and were too young to defend themselves, leaving many of them to be shipped off to new areas. They would wake up screaming in the night after seeing their families poached or culled. In the 1990s we began to learn of the psychological damage done to these young animals and we have considered this to be a form of post-traumatic stress disorder. In more recent years we have learned that the impact of these violent experiences effects the elephant's emotional well-being far more than was previously anticipated. When adults are poached or culled the young grow up without the guiding influence of their family members and are unlikely to learn the proficiencies needed for healthy survival. Add to that the dramatic social consequences. Young bulls have been known to become extremely aggressive and have even attacked, killed or attempted to mate rhino after experiencing traumatic loss.

The basis of their complex society is their communication skills, which are likely to be less refined after such trauma therefore reducing the opportunity to learn the social patterns of an existing, successful family, and deny them the opportunity to learn through role models. Their ability for decision making has an impact on their social behaviour.

It seems that there is still so much for us to learn about the terror, rage and stress that elephant's experience. Knowing this it is not surprising that culling of adult elephants and leaving the young and infant is completely and utterly devastating for them. Trauma does not seem a strong enough word.

Working with children early in my career, I was introduced to two young boys who had witnessed their father stabbing their mother. Stevie was four years old and Joe was six and they were placed by Social Services in our children's centre, with a special request for a dedicated worker to support them. Joe did not talk and would not let Stevie out of his sight for the first few days. I thought we would be okay with these kids and then all hell broke loose. Stevie attacked a younger child causing injury through hitting and biting. We dealt with this incident;

however, over the following days there were similar events with escalating behaviour. Then Joe caught a large gold fish from the classroom tank and skewered it on a pencil. He then ran around the room with blood dripping down his arm, threatening to do this to all the other children. Distressed children and unhappy parents caused our action to remove Stevie and Joe. I felt I had failed them. I had no idea what to do to help them. I did not understand their actions. They just seemed so cruel and damaged. My belief that children are not born "bad" was challenged by my lack of knowledge.

Just like traumatised baby elephants, these children had been traumatised and their behaviours were purely a reaction to what they had witnessed and experienced. Many years later – and having worked with many children who have experienced domestic abuse and violence – I get it!

Just as the elephant calf needs that close relationship with caring adults to survive and thrive, a human child's relationship with the main care giver, and other significant adults, cannot be overemphasised. With a healthy attachment and wholesome parental relationship, children learn to trust, to regulate their emotions and interact with and make sense of the world around them. They need to learn about the world, their safety and value of being an individual. When these relationships are disrupted, unstable or unpredictable, then children learn that they cannot rely on others to keep them safe. When children are abused by a parent or an important adult in their lives, they learn that they are bad kids and that the world is a very bad place.

Most children who are abused, harmed or witness violence will have difficulty in developing a healthy attachment to a parent or caregiver. These children are more vulnerable to stress and have difficulty controlling and expressing their emotions. Many times their response to benign situations is anger or violence. With no secure attachment, their attempts to develop healthy friendships and relationships in adult life may be difficult. These relationships are dependent on learning by example in a family. For children who have experienced complex trauma, significant relationships in adulthood, respecting authority figures and being a parent may be problematic.

Andy was five years old and escaped his abusive and violent father with his mother and two younger sisters by fleeing into the women's refuge. Andy had received regular beatings and had several recorded fractures in his medical records. He had scars on his shoulders from cigarette burns received as a baby and a crooked little finger on his left hand after his father held it in a closed door. He was morbidly obese and was seldom seen without food in his hand. He was a delightful little boy and loved all the positive attention he received from the trained, caring staff.

The first weeks in refuge were wonderful for Andy's mother. Andy became an instant angel. He regularly checked the CCTV cameras and ensured the doors and windows were locked. He worked hard to please all the staff and was very compliant – all very concerning. As expected, this did not last. The police arranged an interview with him and this seemed to create a dramatic change in his life. He returned from the police interview and walked through the house swearing and throwing anything he could lay his hands on. He pushed a TV off a shelf, threw the doll's house, threw open a glass door and ran to the garden where a new wooden garden shed had just been erected.

Andy was now in a rage. His mother was screaming at him to come back into the house, which fell on deaf ears. Andy entered the shed and his small fingers began to destroy the building. He broke the window frame, pulled off the panelling and kicked in a wall. The Social Worker stood helplessly and at a loss of what to do. Even at five years old, Andy was very strong and hard to restrain.

I had recently read a beautiful book called *The Elephant Whisperer* about a farmer (Lawrence Anthony) in Kwa-Zulu Natal who had agreed to work with a herd of nine troubled young elephants. The matriarch was an escape artist breaking through electric fences and unlatching gates. They were destined to be killed if he did not take them. Before he agreed to take them, however, the matriarch and her baby were shot leaving seven human-hating, angry elephants. He describes his work in his book and I remember his just being with these animals, not doing or saying anything – just being. I had tried this with Poppy my traumatised little Dartmoor pony. It had taken three years but it worked.

As I ran down the stairs after being called by the staff to assist with Andy's "outburst", the image of Lawrence and his elephants came to mind. How do you deal with such a violent outburst without doing more harm? So, I entered the wooden shed that was now looking a little like a war zone. We clearly could not let Andy hurt himself or anyone else, although this did not seem to be his plan. He was still hitting and shouting but his energy was waning. And so I just sat. I sat in the doorway so he could not leave. At first I said nothing and I did not make eye contact. He called me all the names he could think of. Shouting out the worst insults his young brain could recall. But I just sat. He made no attempt to harm me. He slowed down, and then crumpled to the floor sobbing. I moved to his shaking body and just stroked his head and hands. He then looked up at me and said, "Sorry I broke your shed."

Whether my actions that day came at a point where Andy was completely exhausted or I was just lucky, I do not know. But, it was the beginning of a relationship with a little boy who hated himself and who was so angry at the world for making him so afraid. He was the target for every playground bully. He was the protector of a mother who was not capable of meeting his emotional needs or keeping him safe. He only knew one response and he used it.

I worked with Andy and his mother for several months and undertook a series of Theraplay® attachment sessions and assisted them to learn a new way of having a relationship with mom as the protector. I think when they left the refuge they were better off for having been with us, but I was under no illusion that I did not have a magic wand in my back pocket. Oh how I wish I did. But I have learned that "good enough" is sometimes all we have. I hoped their relationship was good enough.

The similarities for me between the maternal elephant and my work with children is simple. Be consistent. Offer unconditional love and "show" not "tell" kids that they matter.

A further lesson to be learned from these magnificent mammals is the art of communication. Many human parents make a simple mistake with their children. I know I did when my children were younger. Shouting, raised voices and annoyed or angry instructions do not work. Fear motivated action is not positive parenting. The morning rush of preparations for the day brings much frustration to the average family. Threats of "if you do not get dressed you will go to school in your pyjamas" or "if I am late again I will lose my job", have one effect on young brains – switch off! Calmly trying to explain to a three-year old that running in the road is dangerous and will cause you to be hit by a car and land you in hospital, has little meaning – *what is hospital?* Telling a five-year old that if they are naughty the policeman will come, has its own complications.

I see no evidence of a caring matriarchal elephant sitting her calf down and explaining: "You must stay near me or the big bad lion will eat you." No, the calf learns this through his mother's behaviour – not through lectures, nagging and shouting. If there was one gift I could give to parents it is the understanding that children learn what they live, and not what they are told.

Fear of All Things that Slither!

I don't like snakes! So, since they have played such a big part of my life, I decided to devote an entire chapter of this book to these cold blooded reptiles. Believe it or not Timothy and I were friends. He was a sleek, silver, blind worm about a foot and a bit long with a lizard-like head and no legs. (*Was he a snake?* He moved like one, so that is good enough for me!) He appeared under the purple fronds of my favourite Zimbabwe Jacaranda tree that was my playground. As a young girl my feet were seldom on the ground, if there was a tree to be climbed I was in it and this Jacaranda Tree left a luxurious purple carpet creating a soft entrance to my tree house. I had a bucket on a rope to pull up my booty (usually of the eating kind) into my tree. I had another rope with a metal bar borrowed from my dad's garage. The rope tied in the middle of the bar made a perfect swing for upright or upside down swinging.

One beautiful African day, there I was minding my own business hanging upside down and came face to face with Timothy. *Who got the greater fright?* I do not know. I believe I may have screamed. My mother was always calm is such situations and encouraged my friendship, as it was just a creature with as much right to be there as I had. He seemed to spend much of his time around my tree and so he was named and acknowledged and this friendship of a sort began.

Now, when my older sister Cecily was learning to drive, she would get the keys to my dad's yellow Taunus and practice driving around the lower part of our large garden. This with Timothy's hanging out area, so I would sit on the bonnet of the car directing her so as not to kill Timothy the snake (who may not have been a snake), who I really was a little wary of. The good news was that

Cecily learned to drive; I survived and Timothy survived too.

So, what is it that causes me to be so fearful of snakes? My Timothy experience was not bad! I am not really scared of snakes. I secretly laugh at people in the UK who are irrationally scared of spiders. Whilst many British spiders may be venomous, their jaws do not move in a way that enables them to bite a human. Nevertheless, place a tiny eight-legged predatory arachnid into my office filled with women and there would be a loud and animated response! This of course would put me in great esteem, as I would bravely approach the deadly beast, safely capturing and releasing it far from the office. Hero of the day!

And so one day – after considering this reaction – I brought a collection of realistic fluffy and plastic toy spiders into a training session I was delivering on the subject of "working with children in foster care". I strategically placed them around the room, while watching for responses. Several people moved seats; others made joking comments. They were definitely the main topic of conversation in the room.

What is this thing called fear? Are we programmed to be fearful of spiders or is this about experience? When a child enters his home where his father attempted to strangle his mother the night before, is his feeling of fear rational? Of course we would agree. So why do I dislike snakes so much? I have never been bitten or even touched one. I have had many interesting experiences but live to tell the exciting tails.

In a suburb of Kwa-Zulu, Natal my neighbour, was also my best friend. Our oldest children were toddlers and had many adventures together in our overgrown, wild gardens. The vervet monkeys would ambush our babies and steel any unprotected snack from little human fingers. During this time hamsters were popular pets and my neighbour had one of these. Their cage was getting smelly – as any hamster owner will know – and thus she put it outside for the night. Alas, come morning, the hamster was no more. It had morphed into a slim line, green reptile with a bulging body, which had now become trapped in the little hamster cage. Her frantic call had me rush over to assist in dealing with this event.

Another snake experience happened in the Drakensberg Mountains that lie between Durban and Johannesburg in South Africa. This was a favourite holiday venue when my children were young. All being lovers of nature we would eagerly fill the back pack, each find a long stick (in case of snakes), tightly tie the hiking boots and off we would go.

Shane with snake stick in Injasuti

Shane and Deon with Injasuti Zebra

Krystal was a toddler and was safely encased in a pack on her dad's back. The mountain air was fresh and the sky blue. The excitement of an adventure pulsed through each of us. Halfway up the mountain we found this picture-book cave hidden behind a fine veil of water falling from a fantastic height. Gas burner and kettle were pulled from the pack and soup was warming. Krystal had been freed from her protective nest and was now able to explore on wobbly, inexperienced legs. Out she went through the mist of falling water and down the path with protective mommy in toe. A little way down the path she lost her balance and plopped onto her bottom. As I leaned over to help her up, I saw it…a small, light brown snake with diamond shaped spots decorating its smooth skin. It was sliding out from under a tiny human hand. My brain went directly into panic – fight or flight! Scream or freak out! Her dungaree straps, which lay across her shoulders, had slipped up from her fall and provided the perfect hand-hold to grab and lift. She flew up and into my arms and then I screamed but she was safe.

Back at the game warden's office I described the episode and the offending creature. "A Berg Adder," he explained, "is a neurotoxic, slow moving little snake who was probably snoozing on the path in the sun, known to be quite aggressive." So, why was my precious daughter not bitten – apparently she showed no fear. Had that been my hand with my brain attached, the story would probably have been different.

So, back to fear. The snake did not respond to Krystal with fear. Had he done so, we would have been in some serious trouble.

With experiences like this I guess my fear and dislike of snakes is motivated by experiences. We recognise that animals often cause injury when motivated by fear as do humans.

Many of the children I have worked with demonstrate similar reactions. Fear seems to be the first response for many experiences. Fear being the emotion usually leads to anger being the reaction. Many children (who have experienced trauma or come from hard places) when caught doing something wrong go through a typical set of responses. First defence is to lie: "I didn't kick the cat; he walked in front of me." *He clearly kicked the cat!*

Then he blames the cat: "Well, he is just a stupid cat – always getting in the way." Then they minimise: "Well, he isn't bleeding, so he didn't get hurt."

And then after the final challenge from the parent: "Well, I did see you kick the cat and he is hurting." And then you get rage: "You always blame me. You just like the cat better than me. I hate you."

I imagine this is a common response in most foster homes when caring parents try to correct unacceptable behaviour. This response is motivated by fear and shame. "I am a bad kid." "Everyone hates me." "They are going to send me away." These are the unsaid emotions that course through these young minds. Fear of rejection and shame! Very powerful emotions that generates many incidents of poor behaviour. This is where the family pet is worth its weight in gold.

Consider the greeting you get when you arrive home from a long day. Your cat or dog are at the door – so excited to see you. Tails wagging or the feline-rub against your leg as you try to enter without injury. Would this be the same response from your partner if you arrived home late and dinner was now ruined? Possibly not. But does your dog ever stay mad at you, ignore you when you call or reject you if you forgot to buy the treats?

Here is the magic of working with animals and children. Animals seldom reject. (I say seldom because abused animals may react differently.) They love you for who you are. They are always eager to play or interact – especially if food is involved.

Lilly was eight years old. She was abandoned at a police station as a baby by a mother who had been emotionally unavailable to her since birth and neglected her terribly. Along with her younger sister, they lived with a foster parent for a few years until her sister was adopted and Lilly was put into a children's home. Her survival skills were refined here and when she swore at teachers, threatened to stab children in her class, and threw chairs and books, she was excluded from school. Not surprising. *How do you keep other children safe from Lilly?*

Then a miracle happened. She was seen by a psychologist who made sensible recommendations. She was placed in an exceptional foster home with carers who were angels sent to earth just for Lilly. Together they started to attend therapy with Roxy and me. Many sessions with Lilly and Roxy started on the floor or in the dog basket. Her little fingers would sink into Roxy's fur, her head resting on Roxy's chest. Lilly said she did not have a heart because she didn't feel anything. Using a stethoscope, she heard Roxy's heart and a door was opened. The relationship between Lilly and Roxy was profound in her learning to feel, to be accepted and to recognise that she was worthy of love. Using animals in therapy allows for children to explore without the risk of rejection or shame.

Katie was fourteen in years but only about six in emotional years. She just loved the Shetland ponies. They were super-friendly and very attention seeking. They co-operated when on a lead and loved to be groomed and fed. This was just the recipe for a girl who was smart, and very capable of taking care of herself on the street, yet vulnerable to every sexual predator in the area. Her life experiences had taught her to give adults what they wanted, to survive. Her value was measured by how grown up and sexy she could look and how many boyfriends she could have. Her therapy sessions were designed to build self-esteem and develop healthy protective factors. She really wanted to work with the ponies and her confidence with them increased daily, and she even learned how to hand feed skittish and shy Poppy.

English weather is a challenge at the best of time, but this particular winter was interesting. We had been hit by storm after storm dumping many inches of water on already waterlogged land. Our property was quite flat and what was a puddle soon grew into a lake. Roxy thought the heavens had delivered her a new playground and as any self-respecting Retriever knows – water is just so much fun!

Katie's session this day was taking place in the stables, lights on with the smell of fresh hay, pony poop and mud. Roxy was still learning how to live with ponies and was on a long lead, but the knot became loose and Roxy was free! A flash of white fur drew our attention and there she was, bounding full speed into the new "lake". Katie looked at me and laughed. We ran to try and capture the excited mutt. Wellington boots splashing through the mud met with four chocolate covered, white paws. Her excitement was contagious and so I ran into the water followed by Katie. We ran with Roxy splashing and Katie screaming in sheer delight. Katie was having fun! Roxy was having fun. Heck, I was having fun!

Roxy in her puddle lake

Photo by Deon Chorley

These experiences were spontaneous and delightful and engendered the creation of laughter, serotonin and endorphins all part of the "feel good about myself" recipe.

I received a text from her mother later saying, "Thank you for giving my daughter back – she is smiling." This experience was enabled and enriched by the presence of Roxy and three excited ponies. A young girl experienced delight – a happy moment – for just a moment. No manner of therapeutic training prepared me for this wonderful day.

Becoming a Parent

His little lungs took their first breath and there was the most incredible wail. *I have arrived*, it said and two parents were born. The birth of Shane our oldest son was simple and beautiful. Born on a hot Zimbabwean December morning the world I had known to this point changed forever. We fell in love. The perfect fingers and toes were so enticing we could not resist touching, stroking, examining. His father's eyes filled with tears and my heart simply melted. After just a few minutes the pain of having him taken away to be medically checked was almost too much to bear. My eyes never left him as the medical team did what they had to do. This experience was the most intense falling in love feeling I have ever had.

Psychologists talk about the importance of parents falling in love with their children. This being the beginning of attachment. Bowlby, the founder of the attachment theory, believed that the relationship between parents – especially the primary carer which in most cases is the mother – determines the well-being for that child's future. It is believed that a baby needs this relationship for survival and will actively seek an affectionate relationship. Konrad Lorenz – the author of *King Solomon's Ring* – describes the newly hatched duckling that attaches itself to the first moving objects it sees. In most cases this will be the mother, but if a human were to draw their attention, the duckling would become hopelessly attached.

When Shane was about ten years old, he and his brother were playing in the stream bordering our tropical garden. There they came across a single duckling floating downstream. Catching it with little difficulty, they searched for the siblings or mother but to no avail. Rushing to the house with duckling in cupped hands they presented it to their dad. For some reason he was the imprinting figure. Possibly, because he took to feeding and caring for the little orphan. But true to the findings of Lorenz, Little Quack became Bob's shadow.

Similarly, Shane learned as a baby that if he cried a loving parent would come. If he laughed, we laughed. We learned his hungry cry, his pain cry and his "I need a cuddle" cry. He learned to be resilient when we left a room and to be happy when we returned.

Over the next ten years we experienced the birth of two more children and our family was complete. Watching our children grow up and become individuals of their own brought life's delight and happiness and a bond for us that was unbreakable, even when tested. This connection goes back to pre-birth, a connection that is propped up by emotion, memories and an investment of time.

In my early studies of child development I remember being taught about the early years, that being birth to five years old. A time in a child's growth that sees learning, physical growth and understanding greater than at any other time in our human lifetime. But I have since learned, through experience and study, how vital the time for human connection and emotional well-being occurs pre-birth to eighteen months.

Working in a women's refuge is a unique experience. We often do not talk about such places due to the need for secrecy. Many of our families were at risk of death from violent partners and keeping their whereabouts secure is vital for their survival. That said, this is a place where I have learned about the best and worst of humanity.

A young mother arrived with a two and a half-year-old little boy. She was aggressive, and self-centred, putting her needs before that of her little child. From the start she was unlikeable. Her little boy – who we will call Craig – was neglected and delayed in all areas of his development. He could only just walk, could not talk and did not cry. His hand eye co-ordination was poor and his diet consisted of quick cook noodles, which he would grab with little fingers and shovel in his gaping mouth. He drank coke from a bottle and would just curl up on the floor and sleep anywhere. He sought attention from any stranger who he came into contact with and mimicked other children.

One day as I watched from my office window, I saw a little girl of a similar age fall over and begin to cry. Her attentive mommy came running over, picked her up and cuddled her. Little Craig watched. He then plopped on to his little bottom and made a pathetic attempt at a crying sound. An attuned staff member rushed over to him and attended to him whilst his mother continued communicating on her phone. This became his new game. He was learning.

Now, as I write, it may seem that I disliked this young mother, however, my experience had taught me not to make judgements. She had no idea how to be a mother. She had never been mothered. Neglected by her addicted mother as a baby she slipped under the net and was not known to professionals. Discovered as a four-year-old child living in squalor, her mother was unconscious and near death. Little is known about those four years. Her mother's history drew a solemn picture of prostitution, drug use and abuse. This young women's early days might well have been hell. So, where does the victim end and the non-caring, abusive mother of Craig begin? Whilst I have empathy and sadness for this young mother, our priority was Craig.

I began therapeutic sessions with Craig and his mother as we agreed to work on the basics of parenting and child care. I remember one day, when mum was in my playroom with tears filling her eyes, and at a complete loss at how to play. She had never played. Sadly, just as I began to feel that we were making progress, this young mother attacked another refuge resident and spent the next period of her life in prison, whilst Craig went to foster care and later adoption.

Sadly, I feel that this outcome for Craig was the best we could hope for. But what about that young women? Was her life completely destroyed and was she destined for a sad, self-destructive future? Those of you who do this type of work will understand that feeling of hopelessness that sometimes tries to creep in, but then we quickly close that door so that we can work for another day.

My primary terms of reference are my own experiences. With naturally nurturing parents – who were not perfect – it set the tone for my ability to be a naturally nurturing (non-perfect) parent. Having the responsibility of three wonderfully active, inquisitive and brave children, the adventures were many and the wrinkles and grey hairs well deserved.

Shane was born into a country in the middle of change. As previously mentioned, Rhodesia had now become Zimbabwe with new rules and rulers. We lived in a wild suburb of Harare with huge gardens surrounded by untouched land. Our nearest neighbour was a Minister of Mugabe's government. Their home was up a hill past our large metal gates with a substantial plot of land separating the two properties. This important political figure was guarded twenty-four hours a day by armed guards housed in a small gatehouse.

Now, Mugabe had been our enemy for some years as were his henchmen, and so we had a little anxiety with our new found situation and neighbours. Accidental discharges from their AK47 rifles were not uncommon – or was it just shooting practice? I arrived home with my beautiful new-born baby boy and a new found need to protect. I would die for this little man.

A few days later, I was at home alone when I heard a loud commotion. We had a long tarred driveway boarded by large metal gates and a well-developed, manicured garden. As in most Zimbabwean homes, our windows and doors were guarded by security gates and bars, as safety was a high priority.

Hearing noises that sent fear rushing through my veins, I grabbed baby Shane and locked myself in the safe room, with the smallest windows. We had a party line phone, which meant that our line was shared by other locals and there was a good chance if I picked up the antiquated hand set there would be a conversation already in progress. I whispered down the phone that I had a problem and needed help.

Looking through the netted window I saw the armed men barging through my gates with their weapons in the attack positions. I watched as their large, uncaring boots trampled my beautiful purple irises and little smiley daffodils. This was it. We were done. We were defenceless, had no weapons – a woman and baby stood no chance alone.

This may sound dramatic but considering the history of terrorist attacks on rural properties, the massacres and rapes that were and still are common place and the knowledge of such events having been seen first-hand, my fear was completely justified.

They marched on down the driveway towards the house wounding my beautiful garden. And then my hero arrived. Bob on his white steed; I mean in his white Alpha, pulled up and flew from the door.

"What the hell is going on?!" I heard him shout.

"How, Sir! – There is a snake. It is in your bushes. We must kill it!"

Yes – a damn snake! They had chased the elusive creature from their guardhouse, through the neighbouring bush and into my garden ready for an ambush, attack and killing spree! Whilst I laugh about this incident now, at the time my beliefs and experience was sending very different emotions through my body. It was not too long after this and a few other such experiences that we decided that bringing a child up in the amazingly beautiful country was not something we were prepared for. How your entire view of the world changes when you have a new life that you are responsible for. I was the one in my family who always said, "Never! Never would I leave this place of life and beauty. My Africa." And yet here we were planning to escape Zimbabwe for the safety of South Africa.

Deon and Krystal were born in the coastal city of Durban in Kwa-Zulu Natal, South Africa. Another country with a new set of problems and parental considerations. Moving countries is never an easy thing and learning to fit into a new community with all the subtleties and colloquialisms brought its own challenges.

This is a land of guns, violence, beauty and brave, friendly people – oh and sunshine! The sandy beaches bordering the city were a novelty for our previously landlocked family. This free, unrestricted playground was a place of sheer delight for our kids. From Amanzimtoti and the surfers to Umhlanga Rocks and their rock pools, we explored them all. We watched the shark board netting sharks for the protection of swimmers and fishermen clubbing the colourful squid for dinner. I would distract my children when these fisherman began their killing ritual, as I found this distressing and wanted to protect them.

However, life is not that simple. Protecting children is a difficult balancing act as we want them to learn to be independent and to know how to keep themselves safe. In spite of this, we will not always be there to fulfil this role.

We arrived on the south beach of Durban to celebrate a birthday. Having crossed the busy city road with boogie boards, towels and sun cream, we could safely let the children run ahead to the ice-cream man parked in his regular spot on a large grassy promenade. Our ice-cream vendors had a large freezer box attached to the front of a bicycle. Their precious cargo was kept to temperature with the use of dry ice. A small lid on the top would open and expose the treasure. If you were tall enough you could stand on one of the front tyres and peer in. Two of the three children were tall enough for this but little Krystal was yet to reach the age of ice-cream purchase independence. And so the boys ran ahead to secure their frozen treat.

Something was not right! I could feel the hairs on the back of my neck stand up but had no idea why. The boys were just standing. There was no gleeful activity to indicate the pleasure of their treat. They were just standing motionless. Over laden parents began to run as the boys began to retreat. Poor little Krystal was being dragged along by her little arm. I stood back gathering my brood as Bob, listening to the boy's anxious, excited babble, moved in.

The Zulu ice cream vendor was lying crumpled in a heap with his face in the dirt and his arm twisted behind him. A small, black revolver was dangling in lifeless fingers. The portion of his mouth that was visible was open and a small amount of blood trickled out. The ice cream man was dead! The desire for a treat was now long gone as Bob called for help and I removed my children, who strained their little necks to ensure the details were securely placed in their inquisitive brains.

How do we protect and keep these precious young souls with growing minds safe? Even with the best will in the world this is a task not easily fulfilled. As parents we then decided to avoid cities when on holiday and so time out was spent away from the risk African city life entailed. We were not flush with money and were ever the opportunists and would often incorporate a family break with a business trip. This was one such occasion. Bob needed to deliver some sample kitchen tiles to a client in Newcastle situated between Johannesburg and Durban at the foot of the Drakensberg Mountains. We stayed in a simple lodge at Injasuti and explored the short hikes and waterfalls in the nearby areas.

Packing our tiny car to return home my nose made us aware of a puddle of petrol under the car. The roads going to Injasuti are rough dirt tracks designed for off road vehicles. Ours was a little city car and now a little car with a hole in the fuel tank. The nearest fuel station was back in Newcastle some forty miles along the dirt road. The local warden suggested that we take a shorter path through a local rural village with mud and straw homes and free range chickens, dogs and children.

Travelling over the dirt road and watching for any boulder too large to safely drive over, we still tried to instil a sense of adventure into the children's minds. We were now in the middle of the mountains, miles from any modern life (in the days before mobile phones), completely on our own with a rapidly reducing fuel tank and three oblivious children racing each other to spot the first springbok or warthog. Suddenly, without warning, we became aware of a very low flying helicopter.

Our experience of helicopters took us both back to the days of the war we had lived through in Rhodesia. Even to this day when I hear one of these mechanical creatures hovering overhead, a level of anxiety still makes itself felt.

Rounding a sharp turn and entering a steep valley we saw the event. Political rallies were commonplace in the cities of South Africa during this period. The African National Congress (ANC) was preparing for elections and events were being organised to promote their political viewpoints. The ANC was attempting to campaign in the Kwa-Zulu Natal stronghold and this was often met with resistance and sometimes violence. This turned out to be one such incident. The Inkatha Freedom Party, whose members were now at war with the ANC, were preparing for battle. Unlike the city these rural people were attending in their Zulu war regalia, zebra striped shields and leopard skin loin cloths with sharpened Zulu spears and automatic weapons, dancing to the beat of their chanting voices.

The valley teamed with heaving bodies fuelled by adrenalin. The bulging yellow riot police vehicles seemed as out of place as the automatic weapons. This could have been a scene from ancient times but for these two intruders. And now, our little family filled, fuel-less car was in the middle.

All we could do was try to keep moving as I hid the children under a blanket in the foot well of the back seat. The dark, naked bodies were pushed up against the glass windows and the car rocked to the rhythm of their chanting. The bodies then divided and the yellow beast burst open and armed, uniformed police appeared at the window.

There was clear concern in their voices when they heard of our demise. Two vehicles moved in to escort us down the bumpy dirt road and out of danger. The shrinking petrol tank caused the car to jerk and chug, but going downhill was now an advantage and a blessing. The valley floor plateaued and the danger lessened and the police vehicles evaporated, allowing the little car to roll into town to the petrol station. The news that night informed the nation of a hand grenade attack on a helicopter where an ANC leader was killed.

Such events for any protective parent is so frightening. No one can eliminate all stress or risk from being a parent, but the parent's resilience can affect how the parent and their children cope and recover from life's challenges. The years spent building trusting, loving relationships, maintaining a positive attitude and seeking help as needed builds these skills in the parents, but also in the children as they watch how their parents react and act in any given situation.

The parent-child relationship is so reliant on the ability for both parties to socially interact, self-regulate and communicate emotions in an effective way. Children learn these skills from their parents. Social communication with friends, family and neighbours is an emotional support to successful parenting. The basic needs of food, clothing, shelter, warmth, love and family, are all vital ingredients toward building protective factors for children.

The day Krystal stuck a little bulbous cactus flower up her nose and then used her investigative little finger to securely place it as high as possible, was an example of calling my mother for support and advice. First, trying all that mom suggested i.e. rubbing her nose in pepper to encourage sneezing, when unsuccessful, only then visiting the doctor for prompt removal and anti-histamines. Sadly it seems that this family/communal support is dwindling in our progressive societies. An old African saying that states: "It takes a village to raise a child," seems to hold so much value but has so little attention. Many young parents today seem to be quite alone in their parental journey.

The good news is that there are moments that hold these precious parent-child relationships together, which help us get through the tough times and stay with us forever. The core qualities of being playful parents, accepting with unconditional love, tends to develop trust, giving children the ability to accept guidance and love from parents.

Daniel Hughes highlights the need for playfulness for both children and their parents. Laughter is a way of getting close to your children. Embrace the moment and participate in the reciprocal pleasure of playing and being. These are the moments that hold relationships together. Let me illustrate:

We were not experienced at keeping horses; actually, I had only ridden once or twice in my entire life when I found that I was now owner of three ponies. All my studies had taught me how fantastic these animals were for helping children learn about emotions. So I learned, studied and researched breeds, husbandry and temperament, and that is how we settled on mini Shetland ponies. Simba was six months old and Tigerlilly twelve months when I went to collect them. Poppy, the Dartmoor pony came later. An experienced friend supplied the "horse trailer" and the expertise.

Cornwall had been experiencing severe flooding and the trailer could not access the farm, so the two little fluff balls were dressed in their new head collars and marched down the narrow Cornish lane. Little bigger than a large dogs, we caused some excitement with the locals. Having to stop for cuddles we eventually had them safely tucked into the oversized trailer and headed home.

Learning to care for these wonderful animals was a sheer delight in my life. They stand about forty-two inches at adult height and are strong and intelligent. Their characters were so individual and we learned to read their minds. Now Tigerlilly was the escape artist. With invisible fingers on her lips, she could open any door or gate that had not been securely fastened. She explored any unlocked stable and would eat any unprotected food. The long winter nights in Cornwall mean that feeding is usually done in the dark and usually in the rain. One such night Krystal and I were huddled under hoods, plodding through the boot sucking mud caring for our herd. Unusually, no one came to meet us as we squelched through the field. Alas, the feed stable door was open and in the dark we felt the warmth that comes from their inch thick fur. The electric light exposed three naughty ponies pigging out on their nuggets and hay, but Tigerlilly had shoved her head into a flip lid bucket and it was now being worn as a necklace. In the surprise of the sudden light Poppy, who was always a little skittish, wanted out and barged her way through forcing the smaller hooves and human toes to fight for the same spot. Bruised toes were not uncommon in those early days! Chaos now ensued, with only one doorway, three ponies and two humans were all in the same confined space. But Tigerlilly did not care as she pranced out with her bejewelled neck, kicking up her hind legs in excitement. Now we had to catch her and retrieve the lid. But the two humans were constrained by sheer hysteria. We laughed so hard that it became almost impossible to retrieve the lid. Soaked and energised we returned to the house having had a wonderful experience.

The ability to laugh at life is such a gift and there are many times that laughter becomes the survival strategy. Jellybean was a masterful hunter and would take great delight in showing off his prize by presenting it to the family. One such occasion saw this tiger striped cat proudly deliver a blackbird at my feet. Releasing jaws enabled a rather large bird to attempt an escape. Pandemonium ensued with black feathers filling the room, an excited Jack Russell literally bouncing off the furniture and the humans screeching and yelling. The cat observed – as cats do!

The bird kept trying to fly through the invisible glass and was heading for a concussion. I was ducking as Bob tried to catch it with a towel. Eventually finding the door into the hall, the bird entered the passage and then the bathroom, crash landing under the toilet bowl. The shocked pile of feathers could now be saved by caring hands and then released. The quiet calm that settled on the house was short-lived as all the family relived their experiences, describing their part with much laughter, great excitement and animation, telling their story as if to a stranger.

Many such moments have been shared with my children. When I hear the statement "laughter is the best medicine", I concur completely.

A Boy and his Dog

I was not aware that cats could conceive so soon after popping an energetic litter of six kittens! Hardly had my house recovered from these little furry, delightful monsters when the cat's belly once again began to bulge. She seemed to be nesting in the box of shoes shoved under Krystal's bed again. Wanting to avoid another costly shoe replacement exercise we had just completed, we were too late. Krystal was awoken by little noises from under her bed. This time round we were prepared so we were able to observe and participate in the birth. Not surprisingly mommy cat was quite tired and a little human help was needed. A birth sack exposed a ginger striped belly and a healthy pair of lungs. I wonder if Krystal and Jelly Bean imprinted at this moment?

They became the best of friends. Jelly Bean was like Krystal's shadow. He would sleep in her bed, wait for her to get home from school and sit outside the bathroom door complaining, until she eventually relented and took him in with her. He would wait for her to sit and claim her lap, and he was the one that would bring her a present of the fluffy, sometimes, dead type. She learned the difference between his meows, when he was hungry or scared or just wanted attention. Could this be some form of inter-species attunement?

There appears to be some sort of biological tendency for many humans to actively seek relationships with animals. In ancient cultures, where hunting and gathering was their custom, we can see how relationships formed. Bushmen cave paintings illustrate the animal importance and pays homage to the sacredness of an animal in their culture and how they co-existed.

Native Americans connected with animals in a spiritual way having totem animals as guides to accompany them through their lives. These guides were teachers and offered them protection. The Hindu culture reveres cows as a source of food and a symbol of the earth. They give so much in the way of milk, butter, curd and ask for nothing in return. Thus they are allowed to freely roam through the cities of India, grazing along the roadside.

Early Christianity saw animal involvement. St Francis of Assisi was associated with his love of nature. Legend says St Francis was travelling with some companions along a tree-lined road. He instructed his companions to wait for him as he went to preach to a flock of birds that settled on the ground around him to listen.

Another folklore tells of Francis living in a city that had been terrorised by wolves. He left the safety of the city walls and finding a wolf he made the sign of the cross and instructed the wolf to come and hurt no one. The wolf closed his mouth and lay at Francis' feet.

The 17th century saw the period of Enlightenment, which changed the way animals were seen in society. Humans began to admire animals and beasts were no longer seen as adversaries. There was a slow increase in sympathy towards animals and nature. The practice of keeping pets began expanding from the aristocracy and into the middle classes.

In the 18th century the development of children's literature was seen as a profitable business. Animals were written about where the intention was to engender kindness and moral instruction. Animals were beginning to be used therapeutically and the earliest documented experiment was in the York Retreat UK in the 1790s, where various small domestic animals were kept to aid the mentally ill.

Florence Nightingale is well known for her work in the development of modern nursing and the support she gave in the Crimean War. But she was also known for her love of animals and the first documented attempt at nursing was her treatment of Cap, an injured sheep dog. She had a great love of cats and many letters she sent to her parents described the antics of kittens. Some of her letters were stamped with cat paw prints and even in death her will left provision for her feline friends.

Today we are inundated with the images, characteristics and antics of animals. From birth human babies are exposed to animal characters hanging over their cots, in books and stuffed toys. Many animated programmes are created using animals as the focal point. Advertising companies characterise meerkats, bull dogs, pigs and pigeons to sell their product. Visiting a dental surgery usually finds an aquarium of fish and most homes now have some sort of living creature to complete the household.

This human animal bond is well established in the human history. The need for nourishment and health sees the use of animals for beef, mutton, pork and eggs. Working animals assist in sustaining life and may be a part of general day-to-day family life. Or it may be that their sole purpose is to achieve a task such as the search and rescue dog. Household pets, domestic horses and the use of dogs for rescue purposes all secure the bond between us.

Following the events in New York on 11th September, 2001, there were many unspoken heroes with four legs. Three hundred rescue dogs were assembled and put to work. Their small framed bodies and light weight allowed them to go where human feet could not. These dogs were trained to locate human scent and were able to cover a large area in a short space of time.

A MASH Veterinary unit was set up on site to ensure the welfare of the dogs where their main task was to prevent injury and dehydration and get rest. They found that when treating the dog's eyes with saline to clear dust, the saline ran through the eye into the nose and also cleared the nose to aid in their scenting ability. The presence of these dog in the hellish aftermath brought solace and comfort to those men and woman they came into contact with.

Contact with animals is now known to decrease blood pressure, reduces stress and anxiety and increase our well-being. We learn about nurture and care, patience and unconditional love. People who have animals in their lives are enriched by this connection.

***

Our life did not turn out as planned. Having left Zimbabwe in the early '80s we hoped to settle permanently in South Africa. But the experiences and fears for our children's well-being that formed our decision to leave Zimbabwe were now present in South Africa. So with three young children and little money, we left Africa for the great USA.

Having hired an immigration attorney, we took his advice and travelled around the world to this new life. To cut a very long and painful story short, it turned out that he was a crook and had taken our money and left us in a situation. We stood as witnesses for the US District Attorney, who found him guilty and whilst he served time we were again on the move. This time to the UK.

Now, the reason I tell you this is purely to illustrate the challenges of life. My children had experienced so much loss. Trauma has many guises, and whilst they were loved and protected by us as parents, some of our decisions – albeit well intended – were hard lessons for young children.

Our move to England was a dark time in my life. It was dark because it actually was dark. Arriving in Cornwall in late September was the beginning of a long, grey, wet, dark English winter. We moved into an old, dark, damp Cornish cottage. The contrast between this and my beloved

Africa was stark and painful. We had lost our money, culture, family and we were foreigners.

I guess as parents our actions are sometimes motivated by guilt. To appease this guilt of the loss for my children we agreed to consider a dog. Rental accommodation in the UK does not always allow pets and so we first sought a house which would allow us this luxury.

Twelve-year-old Deon and his father were sent on a mission. As a boy, Deon was a gentle, kind, soft spirited boy and had found some experiences difficult. Their mission was of the four-legged kind. Their return brought home a boy and his dog. The little white ball was cradled in Deon's arms with spotty ears slightly protruding. This was the day a friendship was born.

Twix lived in Deon's room, slept in Deon's bed, left puddles on his floor and ate Deon's belongings. Living adjacent to a cricket field, a common sight was Deon and Twix running on the lush protected green where Deon would fall over and be licked, nuzzled and loved by this little Jack Russell.

As any Jack Russell owner will know, these dogs have spirit and energy. Keeping up with them is a task all of its own. He would run, bounce and dig his way in and out of trouble, often with Deon in tow. He was the master of escape and when set on a particular task of escape, he would have a persistence that was quite enviable. Due to his escape antics we were advised to have him done! Having him neutered was supposed to help with his need for freedom, but to no avail.

We rescued him from a local pig farm after climbing a four foot fence. He was rescued by kind neighbours after exploring nearby villages. He even jumped from a second-storey building, landing in front of a bus and survived – unharmed!

It was not uncommon for us to feel something missing and find Twix was gone. On one such occasion, Deon realised that Twix had again made his escape. He ran across the cricket field and down our quiet road that bordered the new Bodmin bypass. This was a very busy, duel carriageway feeding Truro City with heavily laden trucks and cars crammed with busy people. As Deon neared the bypass he saw the little white dog trotting down the middle of this road. He hesitated to call him in case he just ran in front of an oncoming container truck. Deon feared that he was about to watch his best friend get run over, when the large truck slowed down and pulled over to the middle of the road, thus blocking all the following traffic. Flashing his hazard lights then warned oncoming traffic of the boy and his dog. When the entire road was at a standstill, little Twix excitedly bounded over to his master ready for a new adventure. We often reflect on the actions of the English drivers that day. Was their attention drawn to the little white dog or the running boy? Or is it that English lovers of dogs are prepared to go that extra mile to keep them safe? Which is something we like to think is the case.

Fourteen years later I have a little old Twix at my feet, lying in front of a warm fire. His fur is grey and muscles are stiff. He is much slower and sleeps a lot but the spirit is still there. Deon is now at university studying to be a psychologist and lives away returning home for short holidays. As a parent of adults it is interesting that I still have the feeling that I need to protect my full-grown children from pain. I dread the day when I will be required to inform Deon that his dog has died. We have recently talked about this and together we have planned how I will tell him and how we will care for little Twix.

These connections we have with animals feel significant. Any pet owner will know the sheer pleasure an animal can provide, especially during difficult times. The modern pet is considered to be a part of the family and most now reside in the house as full-time companions. More and more research now illustrates the value of the animal-human bond starting in early child development and moving through life supporting mental illness, physical disability, care of the elderly and in the recovery of abuse and trauma. Specialised programs now include pets when working with incarcerated people or rehabilitation.

In my experience of working in domestic abuse, we have created a specific pet fostering project to assist in people leaving high risk abusive homes. It is not uncommon for victims of domestic abuse to remain in the home with their abuser because they cannot leave their pet, thus remaining at risk of physical and emotional harm and, in some cases, even death. Many of the children I have worked with have been present when pets have been harmed or killed by abusive parents and my job has been to reconstruct the ability to trust.

Poppy was such an amazing animal for this purpose because she had to learn to trust. She was a stocky Dartmoor pony, a breed well renowned in the south-west of England as a hardy animal with great stamina. Yet the future of these animals is changing. Experts think the way to save them is to eat them or at least use them as food for other animals.

Their slaughter is now routine with many being fed to big cats in zoos, which is seen as an effort to conserve the breed as well as their grazing land. A steel bolt gun is pointed at the sweet spot on their heads and enters the brain at 700mph, and within hours the pony will be hanging, butchered and ready for transportation.

This was where Poppy was headed. She was at the auction on the 11th November, 2008 (hence the name), when she was identified as being a pregnant mare and was purchased for four pounds by a woman who wanted the foal. Five months after the birth, when the foal had been weaned, Poppy was off to the butcher again.

I had heard her story and I went to meet her. She did not trust humans. As we entered the field she moved to the furthermost corner with ears back. If you approached, her safety mechanism was to spin her hind quarters around, with some agility for an animal of her size. Her legs would explode out in your direction and her statement was complete.

Getting her into the horse trailer was quite a mission. The only way you could move her was to herd her from the rear, but going anywhere near her rear was interesting. It took several scoops off nuggets, setting a train of treats in the desired direction and five co-operating humans.

She was just getting used to her new surroundings when we noticed a large bulge appeared on her neck about five inches below her ears. Within a day it was the size of a rugby ball and whilst waiting for the vet – it exploded! Oh my goodness – I have never seen or smelt anything quite like it. The vet's examination discovered an infection down to the spine and around the lower neck. We had to pin Poppy up against the wall of the stable with a metal gate as the dead skin and pus was being flushed and removed. It looked like she had been bitten by a shark with a large open wound exposing the tendons, muscles and bones.

How could any animal survive this type of infection and open wound? The vet assured us that with the correct treatment a healthy, hardy pony such as this could survive and so the nursing of Pops began. She received daily antibiotic jabs in the rump, which she hated. Her skin was so thick that the needles would bend and she would simple freak out! A friend mastered a quick, sharp stabbing thrust that impaled her tough hide and delivered the golden liquid. Of course this was not doing anything for the trust building mission we had embarked on.

Three months later Poppy was growing new skin, the fleshy wounds had turned to healthy scabbing and she could once again be released onto a field. Her beautiful fluffy main now had a gap that had never regrown, yet reminded me of the resilience of this special little animal.

Once on the field we started slowly trying to make friends with her. I would take a book and a scoop of pony nuggets and I would just sit. She observed from her safe distance and for many weeks made no progress. I smartened up and left a trail of nuggets leading to me. She would eat to that safe distance and then retreat. Thirteen months later she walked up to me, snatched a mouthful from the scoop and moved back about five paces. My heart was pounding but I did not move. This was our daily activity for a further five to six months. Then one day using the same red scoop, she simply walked up to Krystal's protruding arm holding the treat filled scoop and took a mouthful. Eureka!

Krystal and Poppy

Poppy had set her own rules and has taught me so much patience. She allowed us into her space when she felt like it. Surprisingly enough when we manage to get a head collar on her she would just relent and co-operate. Walking her on a lead rope has always been a sheer pleasure and she was the best pony for grooming, so long as a big bowl of food was present.

Working with Poppy and traumatised children has been a special experience. She did not give of herself easily and the children and young people have had to learn about their own feelings, be aware of their body language, learn to relax and to be calm and not be fearful before the joy of success was experienced. But when Poppy has worked her magic and the child has calmed and has sent the right message, Poppy would just walk over and say hello. What jubilant moments these have been.

A bond with a pet can strengthen the human reliance when experiences are challenging and life is disrupted by death, divorce, abuse, relocation and adoption. The loyalty, unconditional love and comfort offered by a pet is often underestimated by professionals when assessing for an intervention. I have moved into this world of believing in this connection. A connection that enriches daily life as well as working therapeutically with children and animals.

So many of my years have been spent earning a living working with children. Children in pre-school, day care centres, children traumatised by a violent society or damaged by the effects of abusive and violent homes…all through these years my heart has broken at the pain of the trauma I see in the eyes and behaviours of these children. My coping strategy was to go home to my family, both human and other. The relief I have found in the engagement with my animals is profound. Sinking tired fingers into the curls of a doting retriever or sitting with a purring cat on my lap, they ground me, bring me comfort and solace. There is a certain earthy pleasure when you call out to three little ponies across a field and they look up, answer you back and then race across the field to greet you. My intellect says they respond in this way because I am associated with food; my heart says that we have a bond. What a wonderful world to exist in!

The Smiling Dog

Animals and fences! It is surprising how often I am mending fences, whether it is a determined Jack Russell who bites through the wire, a freedom seeking chipmunk or a solid pony butt looking to soothe an unreachable itch – fence repair has become an unwanted talent. When Roxy can escape through a hole in a fence at full speed it is a decent size hole. It was this hole that had me on the field on a cold but sunny Cornish day repairing the fence. The ponies had been given a gift of haylage, sweet grass that is a favourite. I filled their nets to keep them happy and set off on my fence repair task.

Hardly had I arrived at the damage wire when Tigerlilly, a liver chestnut Shetland was at my side. She was super-inquisitive and way too friendly. She was mischievous and smart. She wanted to play – I needed to work. Having cuddled and rubbed and scratched I tried to ignore her. Whilst bending over to hammer the horseshoe nails into the wooden post, I felt a head resting on my back. As I moved, the head moved from my back to my shoulder. Then I had warm lips exploring my face and nuzzling my scarf. I was laughing out loud on my own in a field with a silly little horse. Then I felt those warm soft lips explore my head and begin to groom my hair as she performed with her herd.

I cannot explain the sheer pleasure I felt at that very moment. I was being groomed as one of the herd. I was welcomed and belonged in this field with this animal. I did not want to push her away or tell her off – we were having a moment.

Pleasure, joy, laughter – all these human experiences make us feel good. It is widely recognised that laughter is a powerful antidote to stress, pain and trauma. Laughter helps us to relax our muscles, it boosts our immune system and helps to fight infection. It triggers the release of endorphins and serotonin – natural feel good chemicals. It even improves blood flow and reduces the risk of strokes and heart attacks.

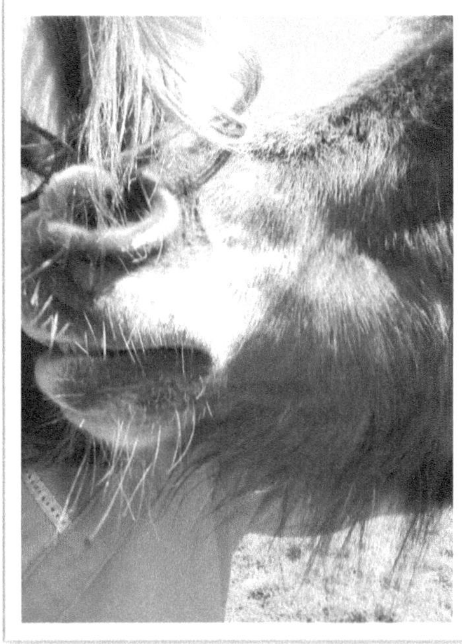

Our selfie – in the moment

Dealing with attempted suicide, self-harm or child abuse in a refuge is no laughing matter. It causes pain, sadness and anxiety for all involved. I remember one such situation when a troubled young woman had inflicted some injuries on herself. When she had been safely placed in the ambulance and was on her way to hospital, I returned to the office and the entire team burst out laughing, albeit quietly. One of the hunky paramedics had split his green trousers whilst treating our client and his pink underwear covered in little red hearts were exposed. As a close team, we laugh a lot and are aware that this helps us to cope with the difficulties of our work.

The ability to see the funny side of life, laugh at yourself and at all that life throws at you, is a powerful survival strategy. This life we have is funny. We cannot take it too seriously. Mistakes are everywhere and can destroy us if we allow them to. I remember trying to recapture my childhood after reading an OPRAH site suggesting that we look back and think about what we enjoyed doing as a child, and then recreate those experiences. I loved climbing trees, colouring pictures and doing head-over heels.

I sized up my king-size bed and decided that this was it. Head between my knees – at forty-eight years old – I rolled onto my bed! Either the bed was smaller than it should have been or I had grown, but I flew off the opposite side of the bed with my legs following my bottom, landing on a very hard floor. I could laugh or I could cry – or maybe a little of both. Oh, but what fun! Yes, laughter is good for us.

Laughing at animals (or is it with animals) is another form of therapy. My therapist has a wet nose and is available 24/7. She is solely devoted to meeting my emotional needs and up-lifting my mood. She awaits my arrival after a busy day with an exuberant greeting, keeps my feet warm whilst I relax and eagerly greets me in the early morning encouraging me to grasp the new day. She shares my interests: a love of the outdoors, walking through rivers, exploring rock pools and running on the beach. She never gets mad with me or tells me off. But when I tell her off she works very hard to repair our relationship. She will drop her head and narrow her eyes, offering her paw in apology and friendship-renewal.

Yes, Roxy has been my therapist. She has given me hugs and kisses, warmth, tenderness, companionship, and has never been critical or judgemental. She has enjoyed my cooking and my smelly socks. She has loved my family with all their wart and bumps, and has accepted and loved each one with affection, while being, oh, so funny.

This large white dog has thrived on attention and has learned that human laughter is a good thing, and thus has led to her performing on her back with her gentle jaws clutching her latest fluffy toy, she would roll around grunting and groaning – irresistible to any human present. When the human is fully engaged she would climb to her feet and chase her flailing tail, bashing into anything that entered her rotating path. The ending of this dance would see her head drown, bum up and a roly-poly back to where she had started.

I have found this sequence irresistible and my facial muscles would respond accordingly, creating an open-mouthed upward movement, often followed by a hearty sound that comes from the belly. This process has created the happy chemicals, and within moments I am feeling so much better than I was.

I have even learned that golden retrievers have a built in smile to match their natural friendliness, as the dark pigmentation of their lower lips frequently displays a canine grin. I like this idea. My therapist has it all – even a smile.

A coping strategy I have mastered in my life – especially working in the field of domestic abuse and violence where we see so much bad in the world – is to appreciate all things natural. The first daffodil poking through on a miserable, grey day. The cry of the buzzard as they announce their seasonal return. The bouncy white tail of an escaping rabbit as it seeks refuge in a Cornish hedge…all these observations bring me pleasure.

Game viewing was one of my favourite childhood activities. Safari is a Swahili word meaning travel and travelling in to the wilderness to observe wildlife was a favourite of mine and is now a worldwide activity where shooting with guns has – in most cases – been replaced with the shooting of cameras.

No longer living near abundant wildlife I have a new hobby. I travel down our urban tracks to a concrete jungle to view the human species as they gather and hunt and meet at the watering hole. Such observation is educating, entertaining and often surprising. Many humans physically attach themselves to other species – predominantly canine – with decorated leather straps and parade them on beaches, parks and coastal footpaths. This group of human's behaviour is somewhat different to the average human, as they seem to stop and greet other humans far more regularly.

Yes, social lubrication is a strange phenomenon. It seems that humans become more comfortable talking to strangers and interacting with others if there is an animal present. This animal presence seems to encourage the initiation of conversation, even with people who may be shy or lack confidence. A human with an animal is more likely to be greeted or even smiled at more frequently. Animals do not communicate with words and so people who may avoid approaching other people may be less afraid to approach an animal.

I now place myself in this group of Homo sapiens. I too walk with a canine attached to a leather strap. I talk to strangers and encourage their children to interact with my canine companion. This activity brings me pleasure and it is not uncommon to end a conversation with a stranger in such circumstance with a smile on my face.

Yes I love my animals. This may be a strange use of the word "love" but I am unaware of any other word to explain the way I feel. It is like a bubbly energy that fills my very being with delight and pleasure – to watch Roxy running alongside the little ponies with the cat sitting on a log overseeing this display, has put my world into a heavenly state. To sit down at night in front of a fire and have a large white dog and ginger cat nuzzle together to share the warmth. To scoop up a fluffy ball of chinchilla and have a cuddle. *Is this love?* Can animals feel this emotion or this this strictly reserved for the rights of humans. I have no doubt I have always had an attachment to my animals. I am aware that they have missed us when we have not been there and behaved in an excited manner on our return. With some animals this may be food motivated excitement, but with others, I think it is attachment. A connection.

When I began Noah's Ark I found myself collecting animals from well-intentioned people. Barney was one such animal. He was a white Netherland Dwarf rabbit who had been kept in a small wooden cage by a breeder who "showed" rabbits. Barney was of good stock and had sired many. But his time was limited when he came to me. He was very used to being handled and I would say that he enjoyed human interaction.

Barney taking medication

I was drawn to him initially as I could see that he would work well with some of the children who came to me for therapy because he was so co-operative. But the more I got to know him, the more I appreciated this little creature. He needed regular grooming to keep his long white fur in good condition and when I went to his pen (he now had half a stable to himself with a beautiful black lady Rex as a neighbour to keep him company), he would bounce to me trying to climb the fence. Lifting him gently I would place him on my shoulder and he would make his way to my neck and nuzzle in with a grunting the showed extreme pleasure. When grooming him, his favourite position was on his back. Not unlike a shark that goes into a state of tonic immobility – Barney would relax and enjoy the experience.

He made me laugh. He kept me company. He enjoyed our time together and he made me cry. When he died my heart broke a little. I felt so honoured to have made the last stage in his life so much better and in return to have known him as a little fluffy friend.

He was not only a loss to me personally and an asset to my business, but he had befriended Tigerlilly. When I left Barney's stable open, Tigerlilly would trot in for a little visit. Their noses would meet at the fence and a welcome ritual would ensue. Tigerlilly would tap her right hoof on the floor and Barney would bounce about thumping his hind legs. After his death, Tigerlilly would hang out at the stable door. If I let her in she would stand at the fence waiting for him to greet her. It was as if she did not understand why he would not come out to play. They say a parent feels the pain of their children's loss; I felt the loss for this little pony.

Whilst I can understand that I personify my animals and create human characteristics in my mind that help me to appreciate and enjoy them, I see that there is a connection from animal to animal that has no human involvement or creation. An inter species friendship of sorts. Whilst considering this I again become aware of my personification of these animals and I make no apology for the views I have of these experiences.

Button's sleek Siamese's fur was soft to the touch. She was a proud cat that ruled the house. But as with all house cats, was selective of what she ate, where she ate and when she ate. Buttons would not drink milk and was picky over her water supply. A dripping bathroom tap was far preferred over a stale bowl on the kitchen floor. Her favourite drinking spot was the goldfish bowl filled to the top and decorated with a golden, moving creature for her entertainment. She would maintain her sphinx like position beside the bowl and tap the smooth glass randomly as the fish approached. But when she went to drink, the golden lips would come up to meet her little curved pink tongue. The first time I observed this behaviour I was sure she had an ulterior motive. Was this dinner? After several years of the same cat and same fish with the same performance, I realised that there was something more here. They knew one another. Buttons was not a threat to the small-brained fish.

Living in the suburban area of Westville outside Durban, visits from vervet monkeys were a daily occurrence. These monkeys grow to about 50cms with a tail that is longer than their body. Their fur is grey with a lighter tummy and they have long arms and legs to enable them to move through trees at some speed. They spend most of their time in trees, but will go to ground to forage or drink. They live in troops of ten to fifty, mostly made up of female and their young.

It was one such troop that spent much of their time in the large Umbrella Tree in my front garden. Their small babies would leave the safety of their mother's belly to explore the lower branches and roof of the house. This activity would drive our German Shepherd absolutely mad. It was like a comical game of cat and mouse or catch me if you can. The monkeys would dive bomb the unsuspecting dog who in turn would respond with loud barking and jumping whilst the little wanna-be humans retreated safely out of reach, chattering and laughing at the hapless dog. Clearly there was pleasure in their torture of the dog.

On one of our annual holidays as a child, we were blessed to stay in the National Parks lodges on the edge of the Zambezi where we slept in the park, where all manner of wild beast roamed freely. The lodges were strategically placed near the great Zambezi River and for several mornings our day began with a visit from the warthogs and mongoose. There is an unusual alliance between these two mammals. Warthogs can be very moody and could easily kill a mongoose, but they also provide breakfast for these little critters. Large, blood filled ticks hang from the pig's bodies – a delicate morsel for the hungry mongoose. Possibly an alliance we can understand as there is sustenance involved.

So how do we explain the relationship between the old, starving lioness who adopted an Oryx calf in Kenya's Samburu Reserve? This was her prey, why did she not eat it? An easy meal that she decided to mother instead. She walked with it, slept with it and groomed it. Was there a greater need she had than to fill her stomach?

Consider the large male polar bears who visit a pack of tethered sled dogs in Canada. Their approach is one of interest, sniffing and looking. The dogs roll to the ground in a submissive manner as bear and dog touch noses. They casually touch, explore each other and then play. They enjoy this social interaction, not as hunter and hunted, but as companions. The images of them playing and interacting fills the mind with awe.

Yes, the need to connect, to create an attachment, to belong, play, to have fun. Whatever it is – it is wonderful.

Animals at Work

Our human-animal relationships demonstrate a form of a co-dependency. Historical finds have taught us how in ancient times animals were buried with the dead. Egyptian paintings depict domestic cats and a Chinese Emperor Ling Ti had such a connection with his dogs that he gave them royal title and associated privileges of the finest food and sleeping facilities.

This connection not only exists for pleasure but also for work and survival. We have mastered the art of using other creatures to do what we want them to; to do what we cannot do; to do things that are too dangerous for us humans and to help us be more efficient.

Consider the African giant pouch rat that is now being used to help clear mines in Mozambique. All my life I have been aware of the death, loss of limbs and life changing injuries these mines have caused to the local people. These rats are no bigger than a small house cat and light enough to move across the land without setting off the mines. They learn quickly and are specially trained before they are put to work with the rat handling team. They are taught to sniff out explosives under the ground and then to scratch around to alert their handler.

As a little girl in Zimbabwe, I remember my dog killing one of these rats and delivering it to us as a gift. We had never seen a rat of such a size before and the family gathered to inspect it. I cannot say I considered it to be a beautiful creature and I am sure my mother was most un-delighted with the gift, but knowing what I know now, I have a new respect for rats.

The United States has a programme administered by the Navy called Navy Marine Mammal Programme (NMMP).

They use bottle nose dolphins and Canadian sea lions to do the same job as dogs – to sniff out explosives from the sea bed. They are trained to find and mark the location of sea mines and return back to their trainer.

An otter is another animal that has been used for centuries as a human helper. These sleek, entertaining little mammals never cease to intrigue me with their curiosity and character. In Bangladesh, fishermen have tamed and trained these animals to work with them to catch fish. For generation after generation the families have bred and hand reared short-haired otters. They are considered a valuable asset and important resource for their business and ultimately their income.

Each otter wears a body harness with a rope connected to restrict the distance they can swim. These ropes are tied to an extended pole, which is moved by foot to encourage the otters in the desired direction. Nets are lowered into the river alongside the bank and the otters are released on their leads. Their job is to corral the fish towards the nets, which are then gathered with the catch. The otters will have select fish given to them and even if the catch is poor, the otter will always be well fed, to keep them interested in their task.

For thousands of years a similar techniques has and still is practiced in China using cormorants with agile fishermen balanced on narrow bamboo boats. Their trained birds have a snare tied around their throat allowing the bird to swallow only smaller fish. Larger fish will get stuck in the gullet and the bird will return to the boat where the fisherman will retrieve the fish. This does seem to be a mutually beneficial activity and the cormorants are not restricted in how far they can go, but seem to return to the boat through choice.

As part of the animal work force modern airports do not only use sniffer dogs but birds of prey also play a vital role keeping the critical take-off and landings free from bird strikes. These incidents are not only extremely costly but are a serious threat to life. The medieval art of Falconry is now being used to protect our runways with these trained, predatory birds that are making their presence felt, thus scaring off the smaller birds. Starlings are a particular risk to aviation and are known as "feathered bullets" as they fly in large flocks and have caused many emergency landings.

One such incident was the passenger plane that made an emergency landing in the frozen Hudson River after hitting a flock of geese with 155 people on board. The collision occurred just after take-off and caused the engines to fail. The miracle on this river was that there was no loss of human life.

To prevent such incidents other methods such as noise makers, poisons and shot guns continue to be used, but the work of falcons and eagles is an important role. One downside to their use is that they cannot work if the weather is too hot, too cold, too windy or too wet.

Even in little Cornwall on the forgotten big toe of the United Kingdom, birds of prey are used. Come summer the little Cornish towns and beautiful coves invite many English and European visits to enjoy the rustic beauty. Where there are people, there is food. Where there is food, there are seagulls. Some consider them to be vermin or flying rats. They dive-bomb innocent holiday makers and steel food from unsuspecting hands, frightening children and adults alike. With revenues at risk action has been taken, calling for falconers to scare off the pigeons and seagulls.

The trainers in Cornwall are kept busy as they are also used to protect the plastic domes of The Eden Project. This is a unique attraction where plastic bio domes have been built in a reclaimed mining pit, to recreate Mediterranean and sub-tropical environments with accompanying fauna and flora. Here Harris Hawks are used to keep seagulls from causing damage to the plastic biomes.

A dog is a common working animal, leading the blind, warning those with epilepsy that a seizure is imminent, opening doors and moving objects for those with disabilities or herding flocks of sheep. Following the 9/11 terrorist attack, dogs not only assisted with the search and recovery of both the living and the dead but therapy dogs were brought on site to interact with the rescue workers to relieve stress and bring comfort. On that dreadful day a guide dog called Roselle lead her blind human down seventy-eight floors to safety whilst an explosive sniffing dog called Sirius lost his life when the buildings collapsed. There is now a park in New York named after this dog.

My wonderful menagerie of animals deliver their own service. Their interactions and behaviours are a daily part of my work with the children and families who have had sad and complicated histories. As the therapist and animal handler, I am required to be very familiar with each animal and their behaviour, to read their signals and keep both child and animal safe. To accomplish this, I spend many hours with each animal, getting to know their habits, how they like to be held, groomed, favourite treat and triggers that may scare them.

I am the one to feed them, I interact with them at feed time, using my voice to call them and I reward them with their food. My presence generates a positive response and a warm welcome.

I have desensitised the animals to loud sounds, quick movements, strange objects and different types of touch. Many children are a little apprehensive to touch animals. For this purpose I use different length feather dusters for the child's first interaction. They hold the handle and stroke the animal with the feathers. The animals are familiar with these tools and respond appropriately.

My goals are determined by the needs of the child and matching those needs to appropriate activities with each animal. The selection of the activity is probably the most time consuming part of the preparing process, as it needs to match both child and motivating factors for the animal. Writing a child's name in hay on the field and then decorating the name with a favourite pony treat is a great activity for building self-esteem. When the ponies are allowed onto the field they do not disappoint as they immediately find the hay and the treats.

Teaching a dog to enjoy catching beef flavoured bubbles delights and generates laughter. Creating an obstacle course for a chinchilla or a guinea pig and using carefully placed treats to motivate investigation, encourages creativity and care taking. Grooming a pony, braiding her mane and decorating with ribbons helps to consider self-care and hygiene. Using a stethoscope on any co-operative animals and then listening to the child's heart opens discussion on love, feelings or even counting and maths. For children who were neglected as babies and struggle with regulation, rhythm helps with this and the process of grooming, brushing, stroking, petting are all calming activities.

Bonding, attachment, making friends, playing, having fun, caregiving, being safe, encouraging vocabulary expansion, use of fine and large motor skills are all outcomes that are aided with animal involvement.

I sometimes wonder if we look for complicated solutions in life when there are much simpler methods if we would just take the time to consider them. Whilst I have a great belief in the connections required to succeed as a human and the immense benefit of therapies to help when life becomes difficult, I think that we may tend to overlook the very simple gift that may be trotting alongside us as we journey through life.

References

Anthony, L. & Spence, G. (2009). *The Elephant Whisperer*. London, Basingstoke and Oxford: Pam Macmillan Ltd.

Hughes, D. A. (1998). *Building the Bonds of Attachment*. Oxford: Rowman and Littlefield Publishers, Inc.

Lorenz K. Z. (1955). *King Solomon's Ring*. London: Methuen & Co Ltd.

Mine Action. (2015, January 21). Retrieved from https://apopo.org/en/mine-action/projects.

Pequeneza, N., Bell K., & Kelen, T. (2011). Hero dogs of 911. Canada: Animal Planet.

The Peregrine Fund. (2015, January 26). Retrieved from http://www.peregrinefund.org/.

Walsh, F. (2009). Human-Animal Bonds I: The Relational Significance of Companion Animals. *Family Process*, *48*(4): 462-480.

Wilson V. J. (1966). *Orphans of the Wild*. Salisbury: Books of Rhodesia Publishing Co (PVT) Ltd.

Glossary

Theraplay®	A specialist attachment therapy created by the Theraplay Institute
ANC	African National Congress – A political party of South Africa
Inkatha	Inkatha Freedom Party – Political Party in South Africa, specifically in the Zulu nation
Veldt	South African name for bush
Voetsak	South African word for – "go away" or "get lost"
Chongololo	A giant African millipede
Gook	Colloquial term for "terrorist"
RSPCA	Royal Society for the Prevention of Cruelty to Animals

*All children's names and details have been changed

About the Author

René Chorley grew up in war torn Zimbabwe, married a local man and had a child there before fleeing to South Africa. There they had two more children whilst René began her career working with children affected by trauma. They moved to USA where she continued to work with dysfunctional families, helping parents to learn  new methods of parenting children from hard places. She completed a Degree in Early Education and Child Development and moved to the UK where she began to work with victims of domestic abuse – specifically women and children in the first instance.

She started the Noah's Ark Family Project in 2010 and has supported children through their hard times, whilst managing a domestic abuse charity, running a women's refuge and opened the first male refuge in the south-west of England.